GLOBAL STOCK MARKET ARCHIVES

Historical Journey of European, American, Asian and African Stock Exchange

FRANK FREEMAN

Copyright

About the Book

In the intricate tapestry of global financial markets, the history of stock exchanges serves as a captivating narrative, weaving together the economic fortunes, cultural shifts, and technological advancements that have shaped the world's financial landscapes. In this volume, we embark on a compelling exploration of the "Historical Journey of European, American, Asian, and African Stock Exchanges."

The evolution of stock exchanges in Europe, America, Asia, and Africa mirrors the profound transformations in societies and economies across these continents. Each region's unique historical context has left an indelible mark on its stock market, influencing trading practices, market structures, and the very essence of financial transactions.

As we delve into the chapters that follow, we traverse through the cobbled streets of medieval European cities where merchants convened to trade shares of ventures and voyages, laying the groundwork for the modern stock exchanges we know today. We navigate the bustling floors of iconic American exchanges, witnessing the birth of Wall Street and the subsequent rise of financial powerhouses that have sculpted the global economic landscape.

Our journey takes us to the vibrant markets of Asia, where ancient trading practices have seamlessly fused with cutting-edge technology, propelling some of the world's most dynamic economies. Meanwhile, in Africa, we explore the resilience and innovation that have characterized stock exchanges across the continent, contributing to the narrative of economic growth and development.

This book seeks to unravel the threads connecting distant financial hubs, providing readers with a panoramic view of the historical intricacies that have influenced and interconnected European, American, Asian, and African stock exchanges. From the booms and busts to the technological revolutions, the reader will gain insights into the forces that have shaped the ebb and flow of global financial markets.

Join us on this historical odyssey, where we illuminate the milestones, challenges, and triumphs that have marked the journey of stock exchanges across continents. Through meticulous research and vivid storytelling, we aim to capture the essence of how these exchanges have become the heartbeat of economies, reflecting the aspirations and challenges of societies throughout the ages.

About the Author

Frank Freeman serves as the CEO of Crypto Research Wave, a dedicated firm committed to ongoing research and updates on global cryptocurrency market trends, providing expert advice in the field. As an American financial market researcher, he champions the application of intermarket technical analysis.

With a vast experience spanning over three decades in trading stocks and financial markets, Frank Freeman has authored numerous books covering Futures Markets, Cryptocurrencies, and Stock Trading. He offers valuable tools and advice for individuals aiming to be successful digital currency investors or traders.

Frank places a significant emphasis on the strategic use of exchange-traded funds (ETFs) in asset allocation, sector rotation, and international trading methods. His financial and stock market trading books have achieved international recognition, being published in eight different languages, including English, Chinese, Portuguese, Spanish, French, Russian, Korean, and Japanese.

From a young age, Frank has actively participated as an investor in prominent financial industry organizations engaged in the development of trading AI.

Contents

1

A Journey Through the History of Global Stock Exchanges

When discussing stocks, the focus is often on companies listed on major stock exchanges such as the New York Stock Exchange (NYSE) or the Nasdaq. Numerous prominent American companies find their place on the NYSE, making it challenging for investors to envision a time when the exchange wasn't synonymous with stock investment and trading. However, this hasn't always been the case; the journey to our present stock exchange system involved several stages. It might be surprising to discover that the initial stock exchange thrived for decades without a single stock being traded.

This chapter explores the progression of stock exchanges, starting from the Venetian states and British coffee houses to the NYSE and its counterparts.

Role and Objectives of the Stock Market

The stock market serves as a crucial avenue for companies to secure funding, complementing debt markets, which are typically more formidable but lack public trading. This platform enables businesses to become publicly traded entities, raising additional capital for expansion by selling ownership shares in the company through a public market. The liquidity provided by an exchange allows investors to swiftly and easily trade securities, making stocks an appealing investment compared to less liquid assets like real estate.

Historically, the pricing of stocks and other assets has played a significant role in shaping economic dynamics, often serving as an indicator of social sentiment or influencing economic activity. An economy experiencing a rising stock market is often perceived as thriving. The stock market is frequently viewed as a primary gauge of a country's economic strength and development.

The fluctuations in share prices are associated with shifts in business investment, impacting household wealth and consumption. Consequently, central banks closely monitor the stock market, overseeing its functioning to maintain financial stability, which is fundamental to their existence.

Stock exchanges also act as clearinghouses for transactions, managing the collection and delivery of shares and guaranteeing payment to security sellers. This eliminates the risk of default for individual buyers or sellers.

The seamless operation of these activities contributes to economic growth by reducing costs and enterprise risks, thereby promoting the production of goods, services, and employment. While there is ongoing debate about whether a bank-based or market-based financial system is optimal, the financial system is generally seen as a contributor to increased prosperity.

Recent events, such as the Global Financial Crisis, have heightened scrutiny of stock market structures, especially market microstructure, focusing on their impact on financial system stability and the transmission of systemic risk.

The Real Merchants of Venice

The financial landscape of Europe saw moneylenders stepping in to address significant gaps left by larger banks. These moneylenders engaged in the exchange of debts among themselves, providing a platform for a lender seeking to offload a high-risk, high-interest loan to swap it for a different loan with another lender. Moreover, these lenders actively participated in purchasing government debt issues.

As their business naturally progressed, these moneylenders transitioned to selling debt issues to individual investors, marking a noteworthy evolution. Among them, the Venetians emerged as pioneers, being the first to engage in the trading of securities from other governments. In the 1300s, Venetian lenders adopted a practice where they carried slates containing information about various issues available for sale and met with clients, resembling the role of a modern-day broker.

The First Stock Exchange—Sans the Stock

Our investigations reveal that Belgium proudly hosted a stock exchange in Antwerp as early as 1531. Brokers and moneylenders convened there to address matters related to business, government, and even individual debt issues. It may seem peculiar to conceive of a stock exchange solely focused on promissory notes and bonds, but in the 1500s, genuine stocks were nonexistent. Various forms of business-financier collaborations existed, generating income akin to stocks, yet there was no officially recognized share being exchanged.

The Proliferation of East India Companies

During the 1600s, the Dutch, British, and French governments granted charters to companies incorporating "East India" in their names. At the zenith of imperialistic endeavors, it appeared that nearly everyone sought a share in the profits derived from the East Indies and Asia, except for the inhabitants of those regions.

The sea voyages returning with goods from the East posed significant risks, including the threats of Barbary pirates, adverse weather conditions, and navigational challenges. To mitigate the risk of potential financial ruin due to a lost ship, ship owners traditionally sought investors who would contribute funds for the voyage. In return, these investors outfitted the ship and crew, receiving a percentage of the proceeds in case of a successful journey. These early limited liability companies often existed for a single voyage, dissolved thereafter, and a new entity was formed for subsequent journeys. Investors diversified their risk by participating in various ventures simultaneously, hedging against the possibility of all ventures ending in disaster.

The formation of East India companies brought about a transformation in business practices. These companies issued stocks that paid dividends on the aggregate proceeds from all their voyages, departing from the previous model of dividend payouts voyage by voyage. This innovation marked the advent of the first modern joint-stock companies, enabling companies to command higher prices for their shares and assemble larger fleets. The sheer scale of these companies, coupled with exclusive royal charters prohibiting competition, translated into substantial profits for investors.

Since the shares of various East India companies were issued on paper, investors could trade these papers among themselves. However, with no established stock exchange at the time, investors had to seek out brokers for transactions. In England, most brokerage and investment activities were conducted in coffee shops around London, where debt issues and shares for sale were either posted on the shop doors or distributed as newsletters.

The South Sea Bubble Bursts

The British East India Company enjoyed one of the most significant competitive advantages in financial history—a government-backed monopoly. As investors began reaping substantial dividends and selling their shares for considerable fortunes, other investors eagerly sought a share in the lucrative opportunities.

The financial boom in England unfolded rapidly, lacking established rules or regulations for share issuance. The South Sea Company (SSC) emerged with a charter similar to that of the British East India Company, promptly listing its shares for sale along with numerous re-issues. Even before the maiden voyage, the SSC utilized its newfound investor wealth to establish opulent offices in prime locations across London.

Inspired by the SSC's success, and recognizing that issuing shares seemed to be the key activity, other entrepreneurs rushed to offer new shares in their ventures. Some ventures were outlandish, such as attempts to reclaim sunshine from vegetables or companies promising investors shares in undisclosed ventures of immense importance. Despite their speculative nature, these shares found buyers. It's a reminder that even in contemporary times, blind pools, akin to these speculative ventures, continue to exist.

The bubble inevitably burst when the SSC failed to distribute dividends on its meager profits, underscoring the distinction between these new share issues and the practices of the

British East India Company. The ensuing crash prompted the government to prohibit the issuance of shares—an embargo that persisted until 1825.

The New York Stock Exchange

The inaugural stock exchange in London was officially established in 1773, a mere 19 years before the inception of the New York Stock Exchange (NYSE). While the London Stock Exchange (LSE) grappled with legal constraints limiting share transactions, the NYSE, for better or worse, engaged in the trading of stocks right from its start. Notably, the Philadelphia Stock Exchange preceded the NYSE as the first stock exchange in the U.S., but the NYSE swiftly ascended to prominence.

Founded by brokers beneath the branches of a buttonwood tree, the New York Stock Exchange established its headquarters on Wall Street. The strategic location, more than any other factor, contributed to the rapid dominance achieved by the NYSE. Situated at the nexus of U.S. business and trade activities and serving as the domestic hub for most banks and major corporations, the NYSE amassed wealth by imposing listing requirements and fees.

For the subsequent two centuries, the NYSE encountered minimal serious domestic competition. Its international standing soared alongside the burgeoning American economy, solidifying its status as the world's most crucial stock exchange. However, the NYSE experienced its share of challenges, from the Great Depression to the Wall Street bombing of 1920, attributed to anarchists and resulting in 38 casualties. This incident also physically scarred many prominent buildings on Wall Street.

Beyond these literal scars, the NYSE faced regulatory changes in the form of stricter listing and reporting requirements during the same period.

NYSE Competitors

Internationally, London emerged as the primary exchange for Europe, yet numerous companies listed internationally were also listed on the New York Stock Exchange (NYSE). Several other countries, including Germany, France, the Netherlands, Switzerland, South Africa, Hong Kong, Japan, Australia, and Canada, established their stock exchanges. However, these were often viewed as stepping stones for domestic companies before making the transition to the London Stock Exchange (LSE) and eventually reaching the premier status of the NYSE. Some of these international exchanges continue to be perceived as risky due to lax listing rules and less stringent government regulations.

Despite the presence of stock exchanges in major centers like Chicago, Los Angeles, and Philadelphia, the NYSE maintained its dominance both domestically and globally. However, in 1971, a new contender emerged to challenge the NYSE's supremacy.

The Nasdaq, conceived by the National Association of Securities Dealers (NASD), now known as the Financial Industry Regulatory Authority (FINRA), was a groundbreaking stock exchange. Operating without a physical space, unlike the NYSE's iconic location at 11 Wall Street, Nasdaq utilized a computer network for electronic trade execution.

The advent of an electronic exchange enhanced trade efficiency and reduced the bid-ask spread, a profit margin the NYSE had previously capitalized on. Nasdaq's competition prompted the NYSE to adapt, leading to its listing and eventual merger with Euronext, forming the first trans-Atlantic exchange. This arrangement persisted until 2014 when Euronext became an independent entity.

In the current landscape, the NYSE, once closely tied to the fortunes or failures of the American economy, has become a global entity. However, Nasdaq is narrowing the gap in terms of market capitalization, challenging the NYSE's historical dominance. As other stock exchanges worldwide strengthen through mergers and domestic economic development, the question remains whether any of them can displace the New York Stock Exchange, the proverbial 800-pound gorilla in the financial realm.

2

200 Years of the United States Stock Market Evolution

The Course of the Exchange initiated the first attempt to categorize the stock market into sectors in 1811, marking a departure from the dominance of three major entities—Bank of England, South Sea stock, and East India Company—in the English stock market during the 1700s. Initially listing twenty securities as a group from 1747 to 1811, The Course of the Exchange expanded its coverage to include various sectors such as canals, docks, assurance, water works, miscellaneous companies, and, notably, iron railways in 1811.

By 1845, the sector classification encompassed mines, bridges, literary institutions, gas, light & coke companies, roads, and more. This evolving sector structure reflected the dynamic nature of the British stock market. As railroads gained prominence, constituting over 80% of the stock market by the mid-1800s, the introduction of stock market indices in the 1800s distinguished between railroads and industrials.

In 1999, the Global Industry Classification System (GICS) was established by MSCI and S&P, initially breaking down the stock market into ten sectors. The number increased to eleven with the inclusion of Real Estate, while Telecommunications transitioned to Communications. The future trajectory of GICS remains uncertain.

GFD recognizes twelve sectors, highlighting the historical significance of transports, which played a crucial role from canals to railroads and airlines. The accompanying graph illustrates the evolution of these sectors over 200 years, showcasing shifts in their capitalization.

In 1791, finance monopolized the stock exchange, representing the entire sector until the mid-1800s. After the Bank of the United States lost its charter in 1836, finance's share dwindled to 20%, which persisted until the Great Depression when government restrictions and the collapse of the banking sector further reduced its share. The 1980s saw a resurgence in the finance sector, reaching over 20% in 2008 before shrinking post-financial crisis.

While transports held a pivotal role in the 1800s, they have evolved into a smaller footnote in the current landscape. Nevertheless, GFD designates transports as a separate sector due to their historical significance. Turnpikes and canals marked the early transportation infrastructure, with the latter unable to establish a national transportation system comparable to the United Kingdom.

The true commencement of the expansion in transports occurred in 1828 with the establishment of the Baltimore and Ohio Railroad. In a vast land-covered United States, railroads had the advantage of reaching places inaccessible to canals. Consequently, from the Civil War until 1900, railroads constituted over half of the capitalization of the U.S. stock market. With most banks and insurance companies traded over-the-counter, railroads accounted for over 80% of trades on the New York Stock Exchange, transforming not only the American economy but also the stock market. European investors engaged in the American "emerging market" by trading American railroad shares on bourses in London, Paris, Amsterdam, and other financial centers. The dominance of railroads in the 1800s was unparalleled, and no other industry has since replicated such influence.

The completion of transcontinental railroads marked the zenith of the railroad network's expansion. However, the advent of automobiles led to a gradual decline in railroads' share of the stock market. While local tramways were absorbed by local governments, national railroads remained in private hands. Unlike European countries where railroads were nationalized, the United States preserved its privately owned national railroads. Although railroads continue to play a vital role in U.S. transportation, they have lost their status as a dominant sector in the American economy.

Utilities, historically playing a small yet significant role, underwent changes in the 1920s. The proliferation of local utilities across the nation led to their consolidation into large corporations, driving the stock market boom of the 1920s. However, the utility sector faced setbacks during the 1930s stock market crash, leading to government regulation and a managed role in the economy. Due to regulation, the likelihood of significant future market share growth for utilities is minimal.

The consumer discretionary sector traces its roots to New England textile mills producing textiles before 1900. Post-1900, the sector witnessed growth with the rise of automobiles and the emergence of large retail stores like Sears, leading to the consumer's ascent in the 1920s. The consumer discretionary sector has maintained a consistent 10-15% share of the American stock market since then.

However, a portion of consumer discretionary stocks has transitioned to the Communications sector due to the transformative impact of the internet, indicating limited future growth.

Real Estate has historically held a less prominent role in the American stock market. The past two decades saw an increase in its significance, primarily due to the efficiency of real estate investment trusts. Despite the challenges in tracking real estate as an asset class, its inclusion as a stock market sector provides valuable insights into property returns over the past 180 years.

Industrials, encompassing businesses producing goods for other businesses, have evolved over the past 100 years. Initially constituting everything other than finance, transports, and utilities, industrials saw their share grow until the 1920s. The sector continued to adapt, with companies like IBM transitioning into the Information Technology sector. Industrial stocks have consistently maintained their share of the market's capitalization.

The materials sector, providing inputs for other sectors, was a major player in the twentieth century. Iron, steel, chemicals, and mining supplied raw materials for various industries. However, in the twenty-first century, materials have contracted as intellectual property and services gained prominence. Materials are expected to continue providing the backbone of the American economy as it leans more towards information technology and autonomous vehicles.

Consumer staples, unlike consumer discretionary, had minimal impact on the stock market until the 1890s. With most people engaged in farming and producing their own staples, the sector only gained significance when large conglomerates took over, providing consumer goods to millions. Today, consumer staples represent a fixed proportion of total output and are expected to maintain their role as a stable sector.

Energy, among the most volatile sectors, dominated when energy supplies were scarce and prices soared. Coal was the primary energy source until the 1860s, followed by the discovery of oil in Pennsylvania. Standard Oil emerged as a colossal entity by 1890, remaining influential despite being broken up in 1913. Throughout the twentieth century, energy held a substantial share in the economy, except in the 1990s when oil prices collapsed. The sector remains subject to fluctuations in energy prices, with its prominence linked to supply and demand dynamics.

ExxonMobil became the World's largest Company

ExxonMobil has once again claimed the title of the world's largest company. Despite the contraction in energy's share of the American stock market due to oil price collapses post-Great Recession, the rise of fracking, and the anticipation of cleaner energy alternatives, the energy sector is poised to remain the most volatile in the twenty-first century.

The communications sector, a recent addition, evolved from the merger of communications and entertainment. Initially, media belonged to the consumer discretionary sector, but the advent of streaming technologies has led to the amalgamation of communications and entertainment into a distinct sector. The birth of the communications sector dates back to the 1860s, marked by the laying of ocean cables, nationwide telegraphs, and the enabling of express services by railroads. Over the past 150 years, the sector has grown steadily as communication costs plummeted, paving the way for continued expansion in the decades ahead.

Two twentieth-century sectors, information technology and health care, have experienced consistent growth. Information technology, originally part of the industrial sector, has burgeoned into a distinct sector propelling stock market growth. The advancement of transistors and semiconductors has been a pivotal force in this expansion, transforming the way information is transmitted, calculated, and stored. The health care sector, driven by the inevitability of mortality, continues to expand as the population ages. The increasing costs associated with prolonging life and the government's role in funding health care contribute to the sector's sustained growth.

The future trajectory of these sectors remains uncertain, with the potential emergence of new sectors and shifts in existing ones. While The Course of the Exchange introduced the concept of stock market sectors in 1811, the number of sectors has remained relatively stable, with only the classification system undergoing changes. The dynamic nature of the global economy ensures that the sector landscape will evolve in unpredictable ways over the course of the twenty-first century. The transformation of once-dominant sectors, such as transports losing its classification, underscores the unpredictable nature of the evolving global economy. As the world undergoes changes, the sector map will inevitably shift in unforeseen ways, inviting anticipation for the future.

3

300 years of the Equity-Risk Premium

The Equity-Risk Premium (ERP) stands as a pivotal variable in the realm of finance, providing investors with insights into the returns of risky investments, such as stocks, relative to the security of risk-free options like government bonds. Notably, a historical overview of the equity premium unveils its dynamic nature, showcasing significant fluctuations from one year to another. In theory, riskier stocks should yield higher returns than the secure haven of government bonds; however, the practical reality has not consistently adhered to this principle.

To delve into the historical shifts of the risk premium, I've undertaken the task of computing the 10-year returns for both stocks and bonds, subsequently determining the variance between them. This approach aims to unveil the 10-year risk premium in both the United States and the United Kingdom. Leveraging GFD's extensive historical data, encompassing over 225 years of stock and bond returns in the United States and over 300 years in the United Kingdom, we can conduct a comprehensive analysis of how the equity risk premium has evolved over the past three centuries.

Stocks, Bonds and the Equity Risk Premium

Figure 1 portrays the 10-year returns for stocks and bonds in the United States. The black line signifies the return on stocks, while the green line represents the return on bonds. It's crucial to note that the data are forward-looking, with the final value for 2008 reflecting the returns from 2008 to 2018. This visual aid clarifies that an individual who invested in stocks in 2008 would have experienced a 12.49% 10-year return between 2008 and 2018. In contrast, a bond investor would have secured a 2.13% annual return, resulting in an equity premium of 10.15%.

Figure 1 distinctly showcases the greater volatility in the return on stocks compared to bonds. The 10-year return on stocks plummeted from 19.87% in 1989/1999 to -2.34% in 1999/2009. Concurrently, the return on government bonds during the same period dipped from 7.98% to 6.40%.

Figure 2 reveals a robust correlation between the current yield on government bonds and the subsequent 10-year return. The black line represents the yield in 2008, while the green line indicates the return on bonds from 2008 to 2018. The analysis suggests that as bond yields decreased from 1981 to 2019, fixed-income investors reaped capital gains that largely offset the yield decline. This insight implies a potential continuation of falling bond yields in the 2020s, given the preceding interest rate decline in the 2010s. While bond yields exhibit yearly fluctuations, they can adhere to upward or downward trends spanning decades. Historically, bond yields declined from 1920 to 1945, rose until 1981, and have been on a declining trajectory since then.

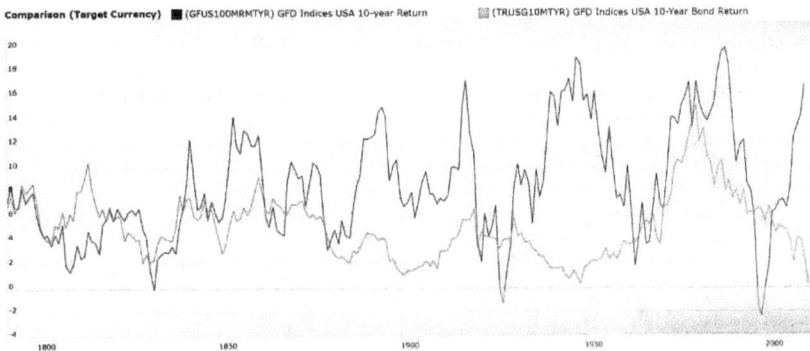

Fig. 1: 10-year returns for stocks and bonds in the United States.

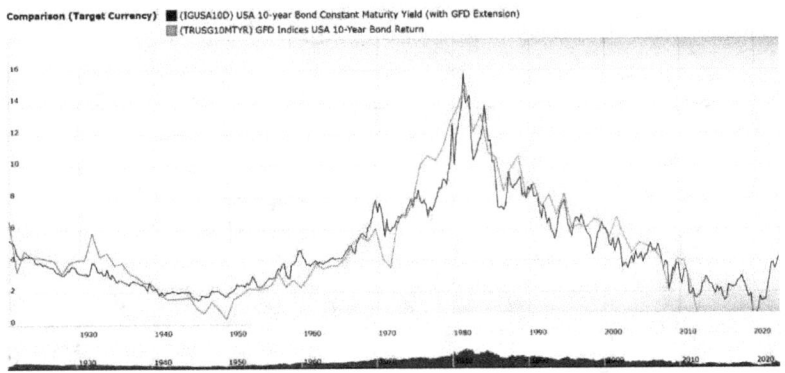

Fig. 2. United States 10-year Government Bond Yield and Returns

Regrettably, no analogous predictor forecasting future stock returns has been identified. Nonetheless, utilizing a 10-year return reveals discernible trends in stock returns over time. Although these trends exhibit shorter durations compared to risk-free bonds, they are perceptible. Over the last century, peaks in stock returns materialized in 1918/1928, 1948/1958, and 1989/1999. Conversely, peaks in bond returns were observed in 1920/1930 and 1981/1991. Lows in stock returns occurred in 1928/1938, 1964/1974, and 1999/2009, while bond returns hit troughs in 1949/1959 and 2008/2018. Essentially, there have been three market cycles in stocks over the past century and two in bonds. Presently, stock returns are following an upward trajectory initiated in 1999/2009, while bond returns are on a declining trend that commenced in 1981/1991. These trends are poised to sustain a positive equity-risk premium (ERP) for several more years, with the likelihood of its augmentation.

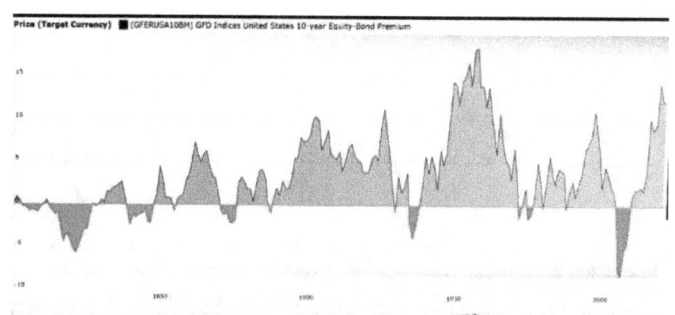

Figure 3. United States 10-year Equity Risk Premium, 1792 to 2008

Figure 3 illustrates the 10-year average equity risk premium, with changes in the return to stocks exerting more influence on the equity premium's volatility than alterations in bond returns. In 2018, the equity premium for the period between 2008 and 2018 was 10.15%, marking a substantial increase from the low of -8.22% in 1999/2009 and concluding a notable descent from 8.87% in 1990/2000. The equity premium has traversed 10-year cycles in the twenty-first century, mirroring the stock market's trajectory through similar cycles.

Despite stocks being inherently riskier than bonds, there have been 17 years within the last 100 years where the 10-year equity premium dipped into negative territory, signifying instances when government bonds outperformed stocks. Over the past 218 years, the equity risk premium exhibited negativity in 59 years. Put differently, bonds surpassed stocks in performance 27% of the time over the last 218 years. The most unfavorable return occurred in 1999/2009, with bonds outpacing stocks by 8.22% annually. In contrast, the highest equity premium was recorded in 1949/1959, with stocks surpassing bonds by 18.17%.

Currently, stock returns are ascending while government bond returns are diminishing. Unless there is an abrupt reversal in the stock market, this suggests that the equity risk premium is likely to continue its upward trajectory for the next few years. However, the reversal of the equity risk premium will eventually occur, though the timing and nature of this reversal remain uncertain.

The Equity Premium in London

Figure 4 displays the equity premium in London since 1700, revealing several notable observations. Firstly, the twentieth century stands out as the most tumultuous among the past three centuries. The equity premium experienced a drastic decline from 4.66% in 1918/1928 to -5.95% in 1928/1938, surged to 16.33% in 1949/1959, dropped to -0.12% in 1972/1982, spiked to 12.94% in 1974/1985, decreased to 4.91% in 1998/2008, and rebounded to 5.36% in 2008/2018. In contrast, the 1800s witnessed fewer dramatic fluctuations in the equity premium. Bonds outperformed stocks in 62 out of 312 years, translating to a roughly 20% occurrence rate. The lowest equity premia were recorded in 1710/1720 (-7.62%) due to the South Sea Bubble, 1928/1938 (-5.95%) during the Great Depression, and 1998/2008 (-4.91%) amid the Financial Crisis. Conversely, the highest equity premia occurred from 1949 to 1953, ranging from 12.99% to 16.

32

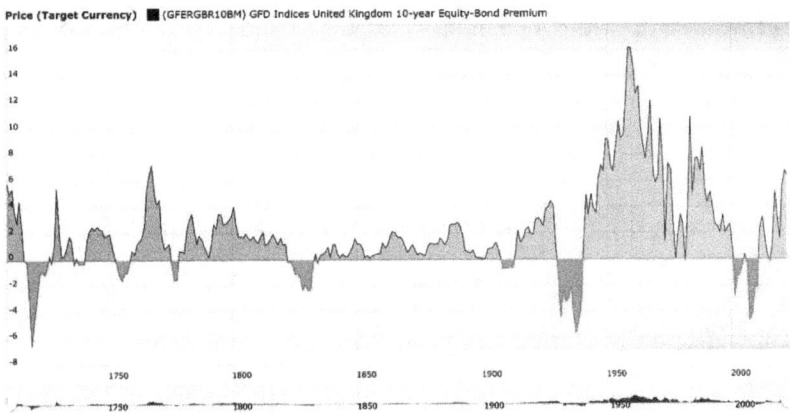

Price (Target Currency) ■ (GFERGBR10BM) GFD Indices United Kingdom 10-year Equity-Bond Premium

Figure 4. United Kingdom 10-year Equity Risk Premium, 1700 to 2008

The similarity in results for the United States and the United Kingdom is striking. The dates of the minimum and maximum dates of the ERP are similar. The ERP is driven by changes in equity returns more than bond returns and equity markets in the United States and the United Kingdom rise and fall at similar points in time. Obviously, financial markets are integrated across international borders.

Into the 2020s; where do we go from here?

Regrettably, due to the 10-year period nature of the data, our calculations are a decade behind. It poses a challenge to predict whether stocks will outperform bonds or the reverse between 2019 and 2029 when returns from 2009 to 2019 are not yet available. Nevertheless, it is evident that the equity premium is on the rise both in the United States and the

33

United Kingdom. The historical trend indicates that stocks outperform bonds 80% of the time, while bonds outperform stocks 20% of the time.

Anticipated returns on bonds are likely to be subdued over the next decade given yields on 10-year bonds being less than 2% in the United States and Canada, less than 1% in the UK, and negative in most of continental Europe. The 10-year return on government bonds is characterized by low volatility. Consequently, the equity premium hinges predominantly on the performance of stocks. At present, the equity risk premium is ascending in both the United States and the United Kingdom, and there is no compelling reason to expect an imminent reversal. However, historical patterns reveal that when the equity risk premium does shift, it tends to persist in that direction for several ensuing years. The exact timing of such a reversal remains uncertain.

Throughout history, the average equity risk premium has hovered around 3% for both the United States and the United Kingdom. Given current bond yields of 2% in the US and 1% in the UK, anticipating equity returns exceeding 5% over the next decade may be challenging. Investors accustomed to elevated returns over the past 80 years may need to adjust to the prospect of lower returns in the remaining 80 years of this century.

Global Financial Data boasts the most extensive historical stock database globally. The repository includes data on stocks listed on the London Stock Exchange from the 1600s to 2018. London served as the global financial hub until World War II, attracting companies from emerging markets to list their shares on the London Stock Exchange before their local exchanges were established. Post-World War I, numerous companies listed on the New York Stock Exchange. Leveraging data from London and New York, we can compute stock market indices for emerging markets during the 1800s and 1900s, preceding the listing of stocks on local exchanges and the calculation of local emerging market indices. This book is part of a series covering such countries.

4

Chinese Stocks Before World War II

Trading of shares in Shanghai predates any such activity in London. The inception of the Shanghai Stock Exchange dates back to 1866, featuring several banks and companies. By the 1930s, Shanghai had become the financial hub of China, witnessing trading in stocks, debentures, government bonds, and futures. In 1937, the Japanese occupation of Shanghai led to the suspension of share trading on December 8, 1941. Trading resumed in 1946 but was halted again when the Communists seized power in 1949. The stock market remained dormant until November 1990, marking the reopening of the Shanghai Stock Exchange. Presently, it stands as one of the world's largest, with a total listing of $4 trillion.

Wenzhong Fan compiled an annual index of stocks listed on the Shanghai Stock Exchange using data from The North China Herald spanning from 1871 to 1940. The depicted market index in Figure 6 suggests robust post-World War I performance, reaching nearly 20,000, yielding an annual return of 7.9% between 1871 and 1940. However, this growth is largely attributed to the inflation that plagued China during the 1930s. When converted into USD, as shown in Figure 7, the returns remain positive but more subdued, providing an annual return of 2.35% between 1871 and 1940, not 7.9%. While Fan's index encompasses a broader array of stocks than the London Stock Exchange, it is based on annual data, lacking the monthly granularity that GFD's China indices offer.

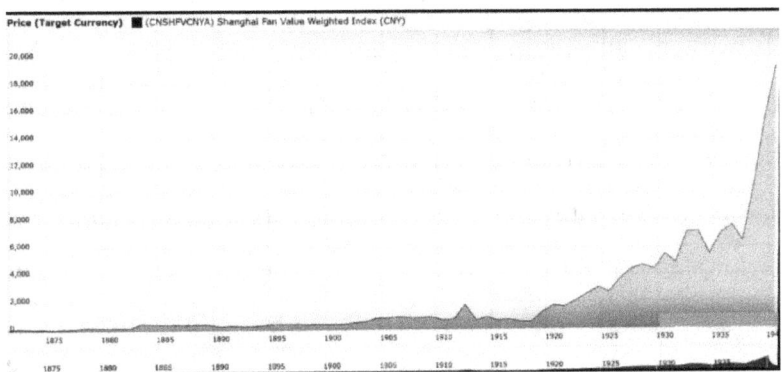

Fig. 6

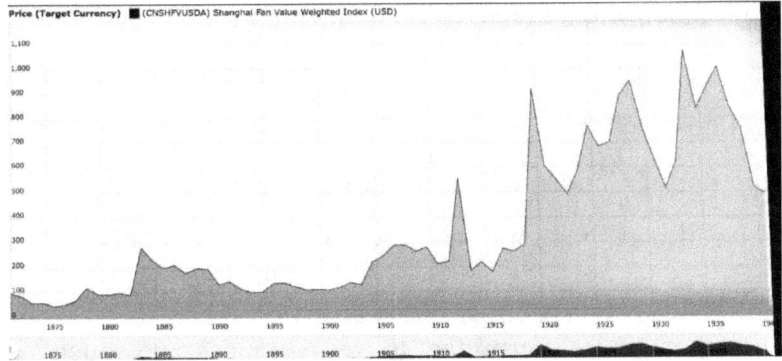

Fig. 7

An intriguing observation from the sectors covered by Shanghai-listed stocks is the omission of railroads, which Europeans desired for exploiting Chinese resources but faced opposition from isolationist Chinese mandarins. Although China experienced a railway boom driven by the government for military purposes, transport stocks were not fully represented on the Shanghai Stock Exchange. However, shipping, canal, and dock companies were prevalent. Surprisingly, Plantations emerged as a sizable sector due to numerous rubber estates around Shanghai. Finance companies, including banks, insurance, real estate firms, and utilities, were well-represented, yet no other sectors stood out as having a substantial number of companies in China.

The Shanghai Stock Exchange, while modest initially, grew from $23 million in market capitalization in 1871 to its peak of $1.7 billion in 1925. However, its size dwindled to $235 million upon closure in 1941. This modest scale was a fraction of China's GDP, primarily because crucial sectors like railroads were not publicly traded, and publicly traded companies were concentrated in main cities where foreigners were permitted to reside and trade, such as Shanghai and Hong Kong.

Shanghai Stocks Listed in London

The data from London span only from 1896 to 1930. In this timeframe, GFD's index of Chinese shares, depicted in Figure 8 below, exhibited a rise from 100 to 158 on a price basis, resulting in an annual increase of 1.36%. On a return basis, the index increased from 100 to 634, translating to an annual return of 5.58% with a dividend yield of 4.16%. This compares favorably with Fan's return of 4.54% during the same period. There was never a grassroots effort to foster economic development through capital markets or integrate the Chinese economy globally. The companies listed in London represented only a handful of entities attempting to develop Chinese resources, rather than Chinese entrepreneurs seeking capital for domestic production. It's noteworthy that, in comparison, the market capitalization of Shanghai shares listed in London was only $35 million in 1925. However, Hong Kong shares listed in London, primarily the Hong Kong and Shanghai Bank (HKSB), amounted to $110 million. Due to China's isolation, British capital had limited influence in China outside of Hong Kong.

Only six stocks listed on the Shanghai Stock Exchange traded in London. These were the British and Chinese Corp. (1909-1930), China Mutual Steam Navigation (1896-1900),

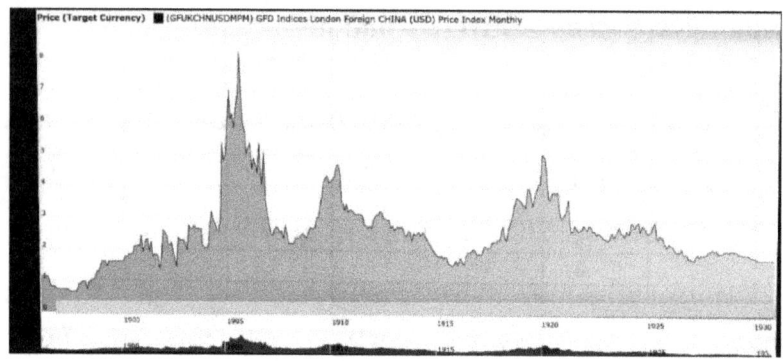

Fig. 8

Chinese Engineering and Mining (1907-1930), the Pekin Syndicate (1900-1930), Shanghai Waterworks (1923-1927), and Shanghai Electric Construction Co. (1924-1926). Similar to most emerging markets of this period, changes in the price of underlying stocks contributed little to the overall return. The majority of returns originated from dividends, necessitating reinvestment in the stock market. The return index for Chinese stocks is depicted in Figure 9 below.

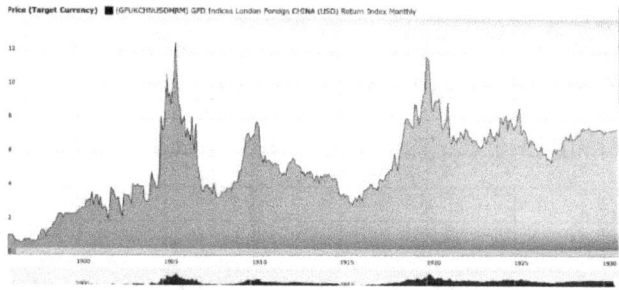

Fig. 9

The Performance of Chinese Government Bonds

The long-term trajectory of Chinese finance is perhaps best illustrated by the performance of Chinese government bonds listed in London. As depicted in Figure 10, these bonds maintained a value above par until the onset of World War I in 1914. Subsequently, there was a consistent decline in the value of Chinese bonds due to worsening political conditions in China and the country's default on its bond obligations. Interestingly, the establishment of the Chinese republic in 1912 had minimal impact on the value of these bonds. However, with the outbreak of World War I, interest rates increased, leading to a decline in the value of Chinese bonds, reaching new lows in 1916, 1920, and 1927.

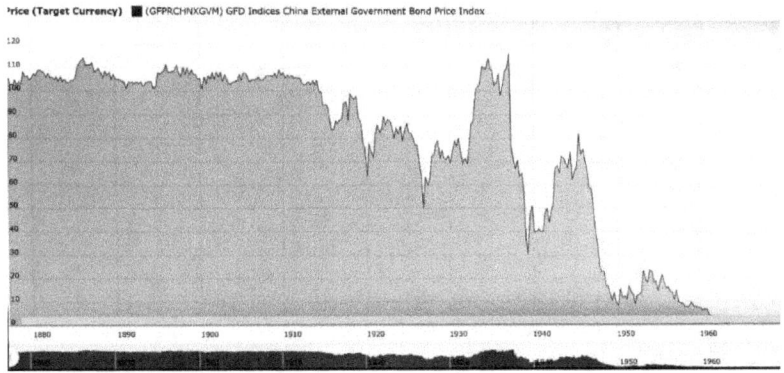

Fig.10

In 1924 and 1925, China defaulted on a significant portion of its sterling loans, but the market experienced a recovery in the 1930s. The value of Chinese bonds rose above par, reaching its peak in 1936, when China attempted to rehabilitate these loans in 1936 and 1937. Nevertheless, the Japanese invasion of China in 1937, capturing both Shanghai and Nanjing, had a detrimental impact on the price of Chinese bonds. Investors foresaw limited funds available for coupon payments, causing a decline in bond prices. Between 1939 and 1945, Chinese bonds staged a partial recovery as investors regained confidence in the Allies' support to help China resist Japanese occupation and address the defaults on government bonds. However, the post-World War II civil war in China dashed any hopes of investors receiving coupon payments, let alone the redemption of the bonds.

Hong Kong Stocks Listed in London

The Hong Kong Stock Exchange was established in 1891 with the formation of the Association of Stock Brokers in Hong Kong. It underwent a name change in 1914, becoming the Hong Kong Stock Exchange. In 1921, the Hong Kong Stockbrokers Association was founded, eventually merging with the Hong Kong Stock Exchange in 1947. From 1969 to 1972, three new exchanges were established, merging into a unified exchange in 1986. The Hang Seng Index, introduced on July 31, 1964, remains the benchmark for Hong Kong after 54 years. However, what characterized Hong Kong Stocks before 1964?

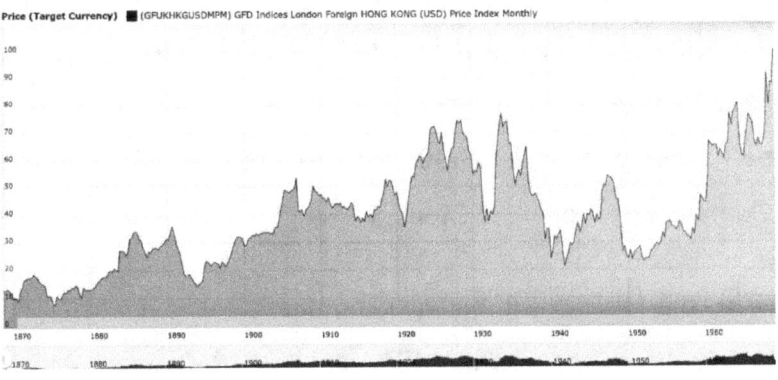

Fig. 11

In 1964, the GFD Hong Kong index featured only two stocks: the Hong Kong and Shanghai Bank and the Indo-China Steam Navigation Co. Interestingly, the Hong Kong and Shanghai Bank had been listed on the London Stock Exchange since 1868, providing a unique dataset for analysis. Figure 11, illustrates the bank stock's performance from 1868 to 1969, spanning over a century of stock prices in Hong Kong, with discernible peaks and declines.

The early 1890s saw a decline driven by the banking crisis in Hong Kong, but the 1895 Treaty of Shimoneseki opening the Chinese market led to a stock market boom for the next

43

decade. There was a rubber boom between 1909 and 1910, impacting prices. The Revolution of 1911 had limited overall impact, but cotton speculation in 1919 and a second rubber boom in 1925 reflected in peaks in the stock market index. The invasion of northern China by Japan in 1931 and the seizure of Shanghai in 1937 led to the closure of the Shanghai Stock Exchange on December 5, 1941. The index performed well in the 1940s but collapsed in 1949 after the Communists took over China.

With the receding threat of Communist takeover in Hong Kong, the index rose steadily until the 1960s when Hong Kong became the entrepôt for southern China. The London Stock Exchange listed shares in Hong Kong companies, contributing to the index provided in Figure 6. From December 1868 to December 1968, the index of Hong Kong stocks rose from 100 to 680, translating to an annual price increase of 1.94%. The return index rose from 1 to 1300 during the same period, yielding an annual return of 7.43% and an annual dividend yield of 5.38% over those 100 years. While primarily tracking the performance of the Hong Kong and Shanghai Banking Corp., the bank consistently provided a level of return to its shareholders. Comparatively, between 1896 and 1930, the performance of Hong Kong stocks surpassed that of Shanghai, returning 2.68% per annum and

8.72% after including dividends, outperforming the 5.58% total return of Shanghai stocks.

It is regrettable that the number of Chinese stocks listed in London is so limited, but it does offer valuable insights into the performance of shares that would otherwise be unavailable. An alternative approach could involve utilizing the Far Eastern Economic Review to construct a comprehensive stock index spanning from the end of World War II to the establishment of the Hang Seng Index in 1964. Speculating on what might have occurred if the Communists hadn't seized power in 1949 remains an unanswered question. The Taiwan Stock Exchange, operational since February 9, 1962, played a pivotal role in Taiwan's technological advancement in semiconductors and other technology sectors. Contemplating how China might differ today if the Shanghai Stock Exchange had never closed in 1949 and if the Kuomintang had triumphed over the Communists is an intriguing, albeit unanswerable, thought.

America's Longest Bear Market

Turning to the longest bear market, we often hear about the worst bear market in U.S. history between 1929 and 1932, where the S&P Composite fell by 86%, returning the stock market to levels not seen since the 1800s. However, when considering the length of bear markets, Global Financial Data defines a bear market as a 20% decline in the stock market and a bull market as a 50% increase. This definition implies that a series of market movements, such as a 30% fall, a 40% rise, and another 30% fall, would be treated as a single bear market. To rephrase the question, we can inquire about the longest period during which the stock market failed to rise by at least 50%.

With the establishment of the US-100 index by Global Financial Data spanning from 1792 to 2019, we can provide an answer. The longest such period lasted 51 years, extending from the inception of the stock market in Philadelphia in 1792, coinciding with the establishment of the Bank of the United States (BUS), until the market bottom in 1843 following the Panic of 1837. During this time, the stock market experienced a decline of over two-thirds of its value, surpassing all bear markets except for the one during the Great Depression mentioned earlier.

5

Banks, Insurance Companies and the 51-Year Bear Market

During the first half of the 1800s, the majority of stocks traded in the United States were related to banks and insurance companies, with most returns stemming from dividends. Between 1792 and 1843, stocks, on average, experienced a 1% annual loss, resulting in a compounded 66% decline over the 51-year period, as depicted in Figure 12. However, if the dividends from stocks had been reinvested, the return would have been positive, with an initial $100 growing to $690 instead of declining to $33. This equated to a gross return of 3.86% per annum, rather than a loss of 1% per annum.

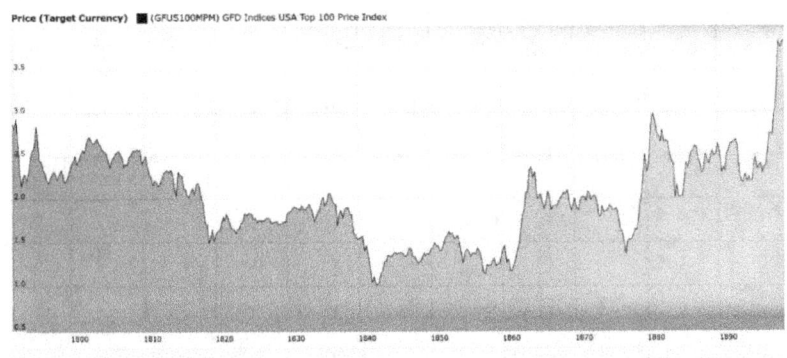

Fig. 12

It is crucial to note that during those 50 years, the First and Second Banks of the United States were the largest companies, representing over 80% of the stock market capitalization in 1792 and at least 20% until 1843. The First Bank rose to $600 before gradually declining to its $400 par by 1815. Similarly, the Second Bank initially saw a price jump to $150, trading between $100 and $125 until President Andrew Jackson failed to renew its charter in 1836. Following its privatization and subsequent failure, the stock collapsed in price along with the rest of the market after the Panic of 1837.

Until the 1830s when railroads emerged, the stock market primarily consisted of state-chartered banks and insurance companies. Most of these entities, located in Boston, New York, or Philadelphia, lacked growth prospects. Profits, if any, were distributed as dividends rather than reinvested. Panics in 1819 and 1837, both precipitated by economic downturns and bank failures, caused market declines between 1792 and 1843.

The Panic of 1819 ensued after the rejection of state-chartered banknotes by the First Bank of the United States and a demand for funds to redeem Louisiana Purchase bonds. The US-100 index fell by 25% between June 1818 and June 1819. The economy recovered modestly in the 1820s and 1830s, but rapid growth led to the Panic of 1837. Factors like the Bank of England raising interest rates in 1836, falling cotton prices, the Specie Circular of 1836, and the Deposit and Distribution Act of 1836 contributed to the economic decline. President Martin Van Buren's refusal to provide relief or increase federal spending prolonged the downturn until 1843.

In the 1830s, the construction of railroads commenced, aiding economic recovery and growth until the Panic of 1857 triggered the next recession.

6

The Longest and Mildest Bear and Bull Market?

The inaugural bear market in the United States was significantly influenced by the inherent nature of the stock market itself. The occurrences of two Panics in 1819 and 1837 precipitated declines in the stock market. However, until the advent of railroads, the limited growth opportunities available hindered the market from transitioning into a bull market. The American economy was predominantly characterized by small banks and insurance companies with minimal growth prospects. Profitable banks distributed dividends to shareholders, while unprofitable ones faced collapse. Consequently, there was an overall annual decline in the price of banks of approximately 1%. Despite this, with banks offering dividends averaging 5%, investors still received an average total return of 4%.

The recoveries from the Panics of 1819 and 1837 were relatively mild, but those following the Panics of 1857, 1873, and 1893 were sharp, as depicted in Figure 12. Post-1840, manufacturing companies emerged around Boston, and the construction of railroads connected American cities. At this juncture, the cyclic pattern of alternating between bull and bear markets commenced and has persisted to the present day. According to our tally, there were four bear markets in the 1800s, twelve in the 1900s, and two, so far, in the 2000s. While the precise number of bear markets before the century concludes remains uncertain, it is assured that no 50-year bear market is likely to recur in the United States.

The Biggest Bull Market over the past 50 years

As the stock market clinches the title of the longest-running bull market in modern financial history, investors are encouraged to focus on the robust fundamentals propelling this sustained upward trend rather than harboring concerns about the milestone.

The ongoing bull market rally, initiated on March 9, 2009, has officially become the lengthiest one on record since World War II, according to S&P Dow Jones Indices. It has surpassed the previous record from 1990 to early 2000, totaling 3,452 days and reaching a historic high. The market has surged over 300 percent since its low point nine years ago.

A caveat exists: if the stock market fails to surpass Tuesday's record and undergoes a 20 percent or more decline, it would result in a tie. The S&P 500, in early Tuesday trading, hovered just below that record and remained flat for the day.

Despite skepticism, Belpointe chief strategist David Nelson urges investors not to be swayed by the milestone, emphasizing that U.S. equity markets continue to exhibit strength and remain a favorable asset class compared to global counterparts. He warns against heeding suggestions to withdraw from the U.S. market in favor of emerging markets, emphasizing the potential pitfalls of such a move.

Market veterans, such as Ed Yardeni from Yardeni Research and J.P. Morgan Chase CEO Jamie Dimon, echo the sentiment that the longevity of the rally is less critical than the underlying economic strength. Yardeni notes that bull markets do not succumb to old age but are more susceptible to recessions, and he anticipates a prolonged expansion. Dimon concurs, suggesting the current bull market could extend for another two or three years.

The current bull market for the S&P 500, having peaked on January 26, 2018, at 2,872.87, has lasted for an impressive 3,453 days, with the furthest decline recorded at 10% to 2,581 on February 8, 2018. Caveats include rounding up a

19.92% fall in 1990 to 20%, marking the start of a new bull market, and the definitions being based on closing prices.

Despite these considerations, it's noteworthy that since 1970, the S&P 500 has witnessed seven bull markets, five of which yielded market rises exceeding 100%.

The Five Biggest Bull Markets over the last 50 years

1. Economic Revival of the 1970s

Contrary to the perception of economic turmoil during the 1970s, certain periods witnessed a rapid increase in assets. A rally commenced in 1974, following a recession that followed the post-Second World War expansion. This rally lasted just over six years, during which the S&P 500 experienced a remarkable 122% rise. Despite the economic recovery, the decade also grappled with high inflation, which could have diminished the gains in asset prices.

2. Bull Market of the Reagan-era Presidency

Among the five bull runs where the S&P 500 rose by over 100%, the Reagan-era presidency bull market was the joint shortest. Nevertheless, on an annual basis, it stood out as the best-performing bull market, with the S&P experiencing a

26% annual rise. Spanning from August 1982 to August 1987, this bullish trend was fueled by significant tax cuts, substantial job creation, and record wealth generation.

3. The Great Expansion of the 1990s

Aligned with favorable economic conditions, robust job growth in the U.S., and a tax relief act, the bull market of the 1990s saw certain stocks becoming attractive. Technology companies flourished with the rise of the internet, leading to a potent bull market that reached extremes before collapsing in early 2000. Starting on October 11, 1990, this bull run persisted for just under nine-and-a-half years, witnessing a total index rise of 417%.

4. Pre-Global Financial Crisis Bull Market

Emerging in the aftermath of the dotcom bubble and the September 11 attacks, this bull market endured from October 2002 to October 2007. Fueled by low interest rates and easy access to credit, a significant portion of which was invested in the housing market, it concluded as property prices began to collapse due to the subprime mortgage crisis.

5. Post-Global Financial Crisis Bull Market

The ongoing bull market stands as the longest on record, initiating in March 2009. Fueled by record-low interest rates and the easy monetary policies implemented by central banks, making borrowing inexpensive, it was further extended by President Trump's tax cuts, reducing taxes paid by U.S. corporations.

7

A Revised Stock Index for Australia

GFD is in the process of updating its stock index for Australia, incorporating data on Australian shares listed in London to enhance the existing dataset sourced from Sydney and other Australian exchanges. While Australia boasts one of the highest stock market returns globally, this figure has been influenced by issues in the indices calculated in the 1950s and the inherent biases in that historical data.

The historical data for Australia, initially computed by Lamberton in the 1950s, is constrained to commercial companies, neglecting returns from mining and finance entities. A parallel challenge is observed in the indices calculated by Schumann and Scheurkogel for South Africa. The inclusion of returns from finance and mining companies in the revised data for Australia aims to provide a more accurate and realistic reflection of the market's historical performance.

The Lamberton Australian Stock Exchange Indices

When Lamberton conducted his return calculations in 1957, the absence of computers necessitated the use of shortcuts, introducing biases into his indices. Firstly, the price indices were unweighted, assigning the same weight to small and large companies. Secondly, dividend data were unweighted measures of yield for all shares. Thirdly, monthly averages, rather than end-of-the-month values, were used in the calculations. Lastly, the limited number of stocks and their rapid turnover, with only 11 out of 40 members from 1920 remaining in 1925, further contributed to biases in Lamberton's indices.

These biases manifested in two main ways. Firstly, the focus on returns to commercial/industrial stocks, neglecting mining and finance stocks, led to inflated returns for the former. Secondly, the calculation of dividends was equal-weighted instead of market-cap weighted, contributing to an estimated addition of at least two percentage points to the actual dividend yields on Australian stocks.

Lamberton's methodology also produced three indices for Australian stocks: mining, finance, and commercial/industrial shares. The mining share index, computed from 1875 to 1910, indicated a decline of 0.80% per annum, while finance stocks rose by 1.57% per annum, and commercial/industrial shares increased by 3.56% per annum. However, by covering the full period from 1875 to

1955, the annual returns on commercial/industrial shares were 4.08%, and for finance shares, it was 1.01%. Incorporating the 6.77% dividend yield on commercial shares from 1882 to 1957 resulted in an annual return exceeding 10% for 80 years, a seemingly implausible difference compared to British shares.

Contrasting this with "real-time" data for Australian indices between 1958 and 2018, where annual real total returns after inflation were about 7%, revealed a stark contrast. By recalculating indices for mining and finance shares listed in London, GFD sought to validate Lamberton's results. The comparison showed discrepancies, such as Lamberton's mining index tripling while GFD's Materials index remained relatively stable during the same period.

GFD has subsequently computed return data for Australian stocks listed on the London Stock Exchange between 1825 and 1985, focusing on finance and mining companies. Combining this with Lamberton's commercial/industrial stock data and GFD dividend data, a more representative data series emerged. Allocating 50% weight to commercial/industrial stocks and 50% to finance and mining shares, the recalculated Australian index showed a price data increase of 3.19% per annum between 1882 and 1936, a notable deviation from Lamberton's 4.66% increase for commercial and industrial stocks. Furthermore, utilizing returns on Australian stocks listed in London allowed the extension of the Australian index back to 1825. This integrated approach provided a more comprehensive and representative data series.

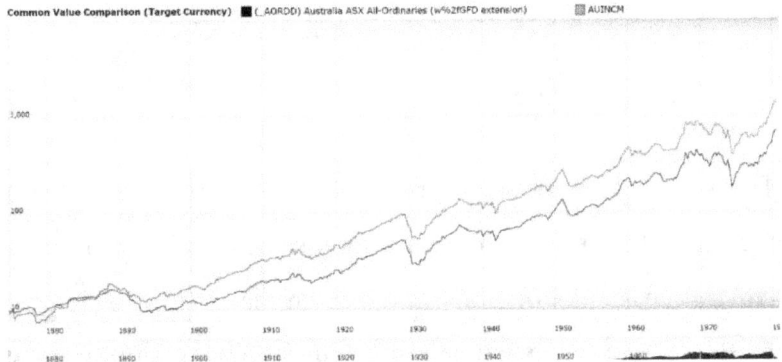

Figure 13. GFD Ordinaries Index (Black) vs. Sydney Commercial and Industrial Index (Green), 1875 to 1980

The data contained in the Australian dividend yield file (SYAUSYM) represents the dividend yields calculated by GFD from the 1830s to the 1950s, while the Lamberton dividend yield data is retained in the SYAUSYQ file. Our approach to recalculating Australian indices involves utilizing the combined monthly Lamberton/GFD data in the Australia ASX All-Ordinaries Price Index (_AORDD) and Return Index (_AORDAD), departing from the previous reliance solely on Lamberton's data. As Lamberton did not compute dividend yield data before 1882, the ASX All-Ordinaries Return index extends back only to 1882. The inclusion of London data enables the extension of the index's starting point to 1825, rather than 1882. The updated stock market returns for Australia are segmented into pre-Lamberton (1825-1882), Lamberton (1882-1936), and post-Lamberton eras (1936-2018), with the outcomes of the new indices detailed below.

The updated returns now appear to present a more realistic picture. Utilizing data from London spanning 1825 to 1882, Australian stocks demonstrated an annual return of 7.99%, with an average price increase of 3.05%, resulting in a dividend yield of 4.80%. Although the Lamberton period exhibits higher figures, they are no longer as unrealistic as before. From 1882 to 1936, Lamberton's data indicated an annual nominal return of 12.09%, which has now been adjusted to 9.48% with the inclusion of new data. While the nominal return post-1936 is higher, much of it is attributed to inflation, as the real return between 1936 and 2018 stands at 5.99%. In the period from 1958 to 2018, the real return is 6.59%. Over the entire covered period, from 1825 to 2018, stock prices increased by 4.17% before inflation and 1.94% after inflation. Factoring in reinvested dividends, the return was 9.77% before inflation and 7.42% after inflation, with a dividend yield of 5.37%. The real return on Australian stocks was higher before 1936, reflecting Australia's status as an emerging market that compensated investors for the elevated risk associated with investing in the country.

In comparison, between 1825 and 2018, US stocks returned 7.10% after inflation, slightly lower than Australia's 7.42%. With these adjustments, the return on Australian stocks is deemed more realistic, leading to the decision to use the GFD/Lamberton data for future returns to Australia. The outcome is depicted in Figure 14.

		Nominal Price	Nominal Return	Inflation	Real Price	Real Return	Dividend Yield
Pre-Lamberton	1825-1882	3.05%	7.99% - 0.17%	3.22%	8.18%	4.80%	
Lamberton	1882-1936	3.32%	9.48%	0.61%	2.70%	8.82%	5.95%
Post-Lamberton	1936-2018	5.53%	12.17%	4.93%	0.57%	5.99%	5.39%
All Years	1825-2018	4.17%	9.77%	2.19%	1.94%	7.42%	5.37%

Figure 14. Australia All-Ordinaries Price Index, 1825 to 2019

In conclusion, Global Financial Data is actively addressing biases present in indices calculated between the 1930s and 1950s, a period preceding the ease of total return calculations facilitated by computers. The approach involves collecting data from companies listed in New York, London, and local exchanges, enabling the computation of returns on these stocks. While historical indices offered the best available information at the time, those calculated for the United States, the United Kingdom, Australia, and other countries suffered from limitations in methodology. These limitations encompassed a small sample of shares, reliance on monthly averages instead of monthly closes, lack of accurate dividend information, and the inability to commence indices at the inception of stock trading, omitting significant decades of market performance from calculations. Global Financial Data is committed to rectifying these deficiencies by generating cap-weighted indices that furnish both price and return indices. Additionally, the calculation of dividend yield, equity premium, and returns to bonds and bills is being provided. Exemplifying this effort are the US-100 and UK-100 indices, showcasing the possibilities that arise from GFD's comprehensive data collection. Australia serves as another instance where historical indices were deemed inadequate, prompting GFD to recalculate indices and enhance estimations of past stock market behavior.

8

Investors and the French Revolution

The foundational narrative of the French Revolution is well-known, depicting France's financial strain due to its support for the United States, resulting in new taxes that sparked a rebellion against the monarchy and aristocracy. The Estates General convened in May 1789, and the storming of the Bastille on July 14, 1789, marked the revolution's commencement. Key events included the passing of the Declaration of the Rights of Man and the abolition of feudalism in August 1789. France officially became a republic in September 1792, and in January 1793, King Louis XVI was executed. The subsequent dictatorship, led by Robespierre and the Committee of Public Safety, ushered in the Reign of Terror. In 1795, the Directory took control, suspending elections and repudiating debts. This regime lasted until 1799 when Napoleon Bonaparte staged a coup, toppling the Directory and assuming leadership in France.

However, the impact on investors during the French Revolution remains a lesser-explored aspect. While the king lost his life, investors experienced significant financial losses.

Pre-Revolution Paris Stock Market Activity

Contrary to common knowledge, the Paris stock market was highly active during the 1700s. Founded on September 24, 1724, the Paris stock exchange saw trading in shares of the French East India Co. even before its formal establishment. GFD possesses data on over 70 securities traded on the Paris bourse during this period, encompassing common stocks, corporate bonds, government bonds, and scrip issues, meticulously recorded from Gazette de France publications. Additionally, Parisian investors had opportunities to invest in stocks and bonds in London and Amsterdam during the 1700s.

Notably, French East India Co. stock exhibited more volatility in the 1700s than shares in London or Amsterdam. The Compagnie des Indes shares experienced a remarkable rise of over 4000% during the 1718-1719 bubble, followed by a crash that wiped out 99% of their value. There were five bull markets with over 90% increases and three bear markets with over 50% declines in Paris during the 1700s, reflecting a market not for the faint-hearted.

The formal closure of the Paris stock exchange occurred on June 27, 1793, with the banning of all joint-stock companies on August 24, 1793. Subsequently, the challenge emerged of liquidating the assets of these companies. Officials from the French East India Co. attempted to oversee their liquidation by bribing government officials, but this effort led to arrests and executions once the bribery was exposed. The liquidation resulted in only three ships in July 1795, causing shareholders in the Compagnie des Indes to lose nearly everything.

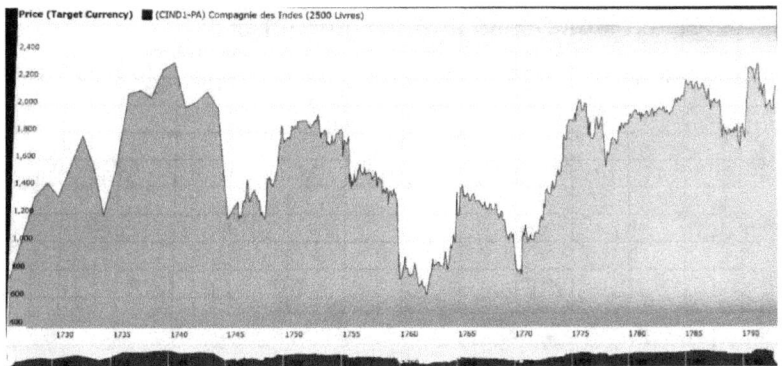

Fig. 15

Bondholders faced a parallel fate. France defaulted on its pre-revolutionary debt in 1796, offering shareholders 1/3 of the value of their old bonds in new 5% consolidated bonds with no interest until 1802. Dutch shareholders experienced a similar loss of 2/3 of their bond value, while English bondholders did not suffer any default.

Post-Revolution Impact on Investors

Investors faced severe losses in the aftermath of the French Revolution. Bondholders witnessed a 2/3 reduction in the value of their bonds, and the official abolition of joint-stock companies in 1793 dealt a blow to investors who received minimal compensation for their shares. Those implicated in the 1793 bribery scandal faced dire consequences, including loss of life. The Assignats, issued during the revolution, depreciated significantly amid rampant inflation in France. By 1796, after inflation, 100 Francs in Assignats from 1789

were worth less than 5 centimes. Counterfeiting Assignats, rendered almost worthless, became a capital offense during the revolution, surpassing other crimes in terms of the number of executions.

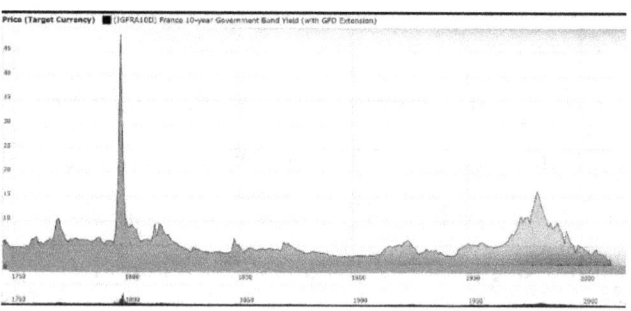

Fig. 16.

The collapse of both the ancient regime and the country's finances paralleled each other during the French Revolution.

Investors found it challenging to sell their shares and bonds, prompting many to seek refuge in England, where their lives were not at risk. Throughout the Napoleonic Wars, other nations, including Sweden, the Netherlands, Portugal, Spain, and Russia, defaulted on their debts. England emerged as the sole country with its finances intact after the wars.

Following Napoleon's ascent to power through a coup on November 9, 1799, efforts were made to restore France's finances. The Livre Tournois was replaced by the French Franc, and 5% Consolidated Bonds were issued to address outstanding French debt. Despite an initial decline in bond prices to 9.25 at the end of 1798, subsequent interest payments from the government led to a recovery in bond prices and a decrease in bond yields. Napoleon's establishment of the Banque de France in 1801 aimed to provide France with a central bank similar to England's. The bank's shares became the largest on the bourse, trading in Paris until nationalization in 1946.

The successful re-establishment of France's finances between 1800 and 1914 positioned Paris as the continental European financial hub, offering shareholders and bondholders one of the highest returns among European countries during that century.

From Uranium to Copper to Silver

Incorporated in New Mexico in 1954, Ranchers Exploration and Development Corp. operated multiple uranium mines in New Mexico and Utah, with the Johnny M Mine in Granta, New Mexico, serving as a primary uranium mine. The company also mined uranium at the Small Fry Mine in Moab, Utah, and extracted cathode copper at the Bluebird Mine in Miami, Arizona. While two mines focused on precious metals, the company conducted placer operations for gold in Alaska and developed the Escalante Silver Mine in southwest Utah, as well as the Revenue Virginius Silver Mine near Ouray, Colorado.

The initial decade of the company's existence yielded minimal results, but a significant breakthrough occurred in 1966 when the Bluebird Copper Mine produced substantial amounts of copper. This led to a surge in stock prices, rising from $5 per share in 1966 to $70 per share in 1967. Ranchers Exploration capitalized on this valuation increase to acquire Big Mike Corp. and expand its operations. The company transitioned from the over-the-counter market to a listing on the American Stock Exchange in 1970, where it remained for the next 14 years.

Sales figures reflected substantial growth, climbing from $400,000 in 1963 to over $15 million in 1971 and surpassing $30 million by 1978. The company underwent 2-for-1 splits in 1970 and 1980, along with a 3-for-2 split in 1983.

The next significant market movement for the stock occurred in 1980 when silver was discovered at the Escalante Silver Mine, coinciding with the Hunt Brothers' attempt to corner the silver market. The Hunts drove silver prices from $6 at the beginning of 1979 to $51 in January 1980, before a rapid drop to $11 by March 1980.

Pay Me in Bars of Gold and Silver!

Anticipating market dynamics, Ranchers Exploration adopted a unique approach to attract shareholders by offering dividends not in US Dollars, but in gold and silver. This strategy mirrored the Dutch East India Company's historical practice of providing in-kind dividends to shareholders in the 1600s.

In June 1981, Ranchers Exploration declared a dividend payable in 2.5 grams of gold for every 500 shares held, translating to a one-ounce gold bar for shareholders owning 6,221 shares. Fractional shares were settled in cash at a rate of $0.0766. The September 1981 dividend continued this trend, offering 2.5 grams for each 400 shares held, and shareholders of 4,997 shares received a one-ounce gold bar. With gold prices at $600 an ounce in June and $700 an ounce in September, the company, with around three million outstanding shares, distributed approximately 600 ounces in gold.

In December, the company transitioned to silver, granting shareholders a one-ounce silver bar for every 120 shares owned. This amounted to 25,000 ounces of silver distributed to shareholders. Subsequent dividends in March and June 1982, payable in silver, were set at a rate of 1 ounce for every 120 shares, while the September 1982 dividend adjusted to 1 ounce for each 100 shares. The December 1982 dividend reverted to gold, offering 1 ounce for every 4,977 shares. Throughout 1983 and 1984, dividends continued in silver, with rates set at 1 ounce for every 100 shares and 150 shares, respectively.

Investors, seeking refuge from inflationary pressures eroding the value of dollars, flocked to the stock. Ranchers Exploration's share price mirrored the fluctuations in gold and silver prices, plummeting from over $65 in April 1981 to $12.50 in March 1982, then surging to $53 ($35.25 post the 3-for-2 split) in April 1984.

Recognizing the value in Ranchers Exploration, Hecla Mining acquired the company on July 27, 1984. Shareholders received 1.55 shares of Hecla Mining Co. common stock, equivalent to approximately $21 in cash. While Hecla Mining continued dividend payouts in cash, not in precious metals, former Ranchers Exploration shareholders likely retained bars of gold and silver received as dividends during the unconventional payment era.

9

LONDON STOCK EXCHANGE

The Investors Monthly Manual (IMM), an archival resource from The London Exchange spanning the years 1871 to 1930, provides a comprehensive snapshot of the bustling financial activity during the colonial era. This period marked the zenith of the London market's prominence, serving as the world's most active marketplace. Beyond domestic securities, it facilitated the trading of sovereign debt from across the globe, encompassing both equity and debt instruments of foreign companies. The IMM meticulously documents prices, dividends, capitalization figures, and other potentially valuable information. The articles within the IMM delve into issues relevant to investors throughout the 70-year duration.

To enhance accessibility for scholars, the ICF (International Center of Finance) secured a grant from a benevolent donor to digitize this data into an electronic database. Scholars can now download, manipulate, and analyze the scanned issues of the IMM directly from the website. The database is available for download either as a whole or in specific series.

Professors William Goetzmann and K. Geert Rouwenhorst extend an invitation to scholars who have utilized or inputted data related to this project to share their findings on the site. Additionally, they welcome information regarding relevant references associated with the database.

Moving beyond London, the NYSE History Research Project is an ongoing initiative by the International Center of Finance to accumulate price and dividend information on NYSE stocks from its inception to the present. This effort aims to facilitate the analysis of long-term trends and performance on the New York Stock Exchange.

Similarly, the Shanghai Stock Exchange History Research Project, conducted by Professors Christos Cabolis, Wenzhong Fan, William Goetzmann, and Siew Choo (Julie) Ng, focuses on gathering price and dividend data for stocks listed on the Shanghai Stock Exchange (SSE) during the nineteenth and early twentieth centuries. The project traces the development of the securities market in Shanghai from the late 1860s until its temporary cessation on December 8, 1941, due to the Japanese occupation of the International Settlement. The dataset, primarily sourced from The North-China Herald, an English newspaper in Shanghai, spans from 1870 to 1940, enabling a comprehensive examination of long-term trends and performance on the SSE.

St. Petersburg Stock Exchange Project

Delving into the history of the St. Petersburg Stock Exchange (SPSE) spanning from 1865 to 1917, the ongoing St. Petersburg Stock Exchange History Research Project is a collaborative effort by the International Center of Finance. Led by researchers William Goetzmann, Christos Cabolis, and Peter Radchenko, the initiative aims to amass price and dividend information for stocks listed on the SPSE during the nineteenth and early twentieth centuries.

Monthly price data has been meticulously compiled for all securities listed on the St. Petersburg Stock Exchange, covering the period from January 1865 to July 1914. The Stock Exchange temporarily closed during World War I but reopened for two months in 1917 before shutting down again for a prolonged 74-year hiatus following the 1917 revolution. The primary objective of this project is to construct comprehensive data series for the SPSE, enabling the International Center of Finance to explore long-term trends and performance.

South Sea Bubble 1720 Project

The inaugural global financial bubble unfolded in 1720 across Paris, London, and the Netherlands. Researchers William Goetzmann, Geert Rouwenhorst, and Rik Frehen have meticulously gathered stock prices for numerous traded companies during this period. The dataset encompasses Dutch firms quoted in markets in the Netherlands, British firms quoted in the Netherlands, and previously unstudied British firms quoted in London. Additional British price information from Larry Neal has been incorporated into the database, which also features international exchange rates and the Agio of the Bank of Amsterdam.

Cowles Data

Established in 1932, the Cowles Commission for Research in Economics is a non-profit organization dedicated to conducting and promoting investigations into economic problems. Affiliated with the Econometric Society, the commission issues papers and monographs of econometric or economic-statistical nature. These publications contribute to the advancement of economic theory in its connection to statistics and mathematics, showcasing the interdisciplinary nature of the Cowles Commission's work.

10

History of African Stock Exchanges

The origins of African stock exchanges can be traced back to the late 19th century when the inaugural stock exchange was established in South Africa in 1887. Subsequently, numerous other exchanges emerged across the continent, with the majority of them taking shape in the 20th century.

In 1906, the Johannesburg Stock Exchange (JSE) was established in South Africa, marking the continent's first publicly traded stock exchange. Swiftly ascending to become Africa's largest stock exchange, the JSE continues to hold significant prominence today.

In 1913, the Cairo & Alexandria Stock Exchange was founded in Egypt, becoming the first stock exchange in the Middle East and North Africa. Initially focused on trading shares of the Suez Canal Company, it later expanded its scope to include various securities.

Despite their significant contributions to the global economy, they have often been overlooked in mainstream discussions of financial markets. However, the rise of emerging markets in recent years has led to a renewed interest in the history and development of African stock exchanges. In this book, we will explore the rich history of African stock exchanges, from their origins to their current status as important players in the global financial landscape. We will also examine the challenges facing African stock exchanges today and the opportunities that lie ahead for these dynamic and exciting markets. Join us on this journey of discovery and learn about the fascinating history of African stock exchanges.

The significance of African stock exchanges in the global context

African stock exchanges may not often come to mind when discussing global financial markets, but their significance should not be overlooked. These exchanges play a vital role in shaping the economic landscape of the African continent and contribute to the overall development and growth of African economies.

Historically, African stock exchanges have faced a multitude of challenges, including political instability, limited liquidity, and a lack of investor confidence. However, in recent years, there has been a notable shift as these exchanges have gradually gained momentum and started attracting both local and international investors.

One of the key reasons why African stock exchanges are increasingly gaining attention is the continent's rapid economic growth. With a rising middle class, expanding consumer markets, and a growing focus on infrastructure development, African economies are emerging as attractive investment destinations. As a result, African stock exchanges have become platforms for businesses to raise capital, facilitate trade, and generate wealth.

Moreover, African stock exchanges are not just limited to major financial hubs like Johannesburg or Nairobi. They are spread across the continent, serving as catalysts for regional economic integration. These exchanges provide opportunities for local businesses to access capital markets, fueling entrepreneurship and innovation.

Additionally, African stock exchanges offer a unique chance for investors to diversify their portfolios and tap into markets with high growth potential. These exchanges provide a gateway to sectors such as telecommunications, banking, agriculture, and natural resources, which are driving economic expansion in Africa.

In this book, we will delve into the rich history, evolution, and current state of African stock exchanges. We will explore how these exchanges have overcome challenges, adapted to changing dynamics, and positioned themselves as key players in the global financial landscape. Join us as we unlock the past and gain a deeper understanding of the fascinating journey of African stock exchanges.

Pre-colonial trading practices and early financial systems in Africa

To truly understand the history of African stock exchanges, it is crucial to delve into the pre-colonial era and explore the early trading practices and financial systems that laid the foundation for these exchanges. Before the arrival of European colonial powers, Africa had a rich and diverse trading landscape, with various sophisticated economic systems in place.

One notable aspect of pre-colonial trading practices in Africa was the existence of vibrant marketplaces. These marketplaces served as central hubs for trade, where goods, services, and even currencies were exchanged. These markets facilitated not only local trade but also long-distance trade routes that stretched across the continent. The Trans-Saharan trade routes, for example, connected West Africa with North Africa and the Middle East, fostering economic growth and cultural exchange.

In addition to the physical marketplaces, Africa had its own unique financial systems that were deeply rooted in the local cultures and traditions. One such system was the use of cowrie shells as a form of currency. Cowrie shells, which were abundant in coastal regions, served as a widely accepted medium of exchange. They were used for various transactions, including trade, dowries, and even as a symbol of wealth and status.

Furthermore, many African societies had intricate credit and lending systems in place. Traditional credit associations, known as "susu" or "esusu" in West Africa, allowed individuals to pool their resources and provide financial support to one another. These systems were based on trust, reciprocity, and community cohesion, providing a sense of financial security and stability.

While these pre-colonial trading practices and financial systems were not structured like modern stock exchanges, they laid the groundwork for future economic development and the emergence of formal stock markets in Africa. These historical practices and systems highlight the resilience and ingenuity of African societies in navigating complex economic landscapes long before the arrival of external influences.

Understanding this rich pre-colonial history is essential in appreciating the significance of African stock exchanges today. It sheds light on the continent's ability to adapt and innovate within the global financial arena, and serves as a reminder of the enduring legacy of Africa's economic heritage.

Colonial impact: The establishment of stock exchanges by European powers

The establishment of stock exchanges by European powers had a significant colonial impact on African countries. During the era of European colonization, various European powers sought to exploit the rich resources and economic potential of Africa. As part of their economic dominance and control, these colonial powers introduced stock exchanges in many African territories.

The establishment of stock exchanges served multiple purposes for the colonizers. Firstly, it provided a platform for European investors and companies to access African markets and resources, facilitating the extraction of wealth from the continent. Additionally, it allowed the colonizers to exert control over the economic activities of the African territories, ensuring that profits flowed back to the colonial powers.

However, the impact of these stock exchanges was not solely beneficial for the colonizers. While they facilitated economic activities, they also perpetuated the economic inequalities and exploitative systems that were characteristic of the colonial era. African populations were often excluded from participating in these stock exchanges, further marginalizing them and limiting their economic opportunities.

Furthermore, the establishment of stock exchanges by European powers contributed to the financial dependency of African countries on their colonizers. The functioning of these exchanges was closely tied to the interests of the European colonial powers, and their control over the financial systems of African nations continued even after independence.

Today, the legacy of these colonial-era stock exchanges is still apparent in many African countries. The structures and regulations put in place by the colonizers continue to shape the functioning of the stock markets, with some countries still grappling with the challenges of economic dependency and limited local participation.

Understanding the colonial impact on the establishment of stock exchanges in Africa is crucial for comprehending the complex economic history of the continent. It highlights the historical dynamics of power, exploitation, and economic control, and sheds light on the ongoing efforts to reshape and reclaim African financial systems for the benefit of their own populations.

Post-independence development of African stock exchanges

The post-independence development of African stock exchanges marks a pivotal turning point in the economic landscape of the continent. As African nations gained independence from colonial rule, they faced numerous challenges in establishing and developing their own financial systems. One of the key components of this process was the creation and growth of stock exchanges.

In the years following independence, many African countries recognized the importance of having a stock exchange as a crucial element of their economic infrastructure. These exchanges provided a platform for companies to raise capital, facilitate investment, and foster economic growth. Moreover, they played a significant role in attracting foreign investors, encouraging entrepreneurship, and promoting domestic industries.

The establishment of stock exchanges in various African countries was often met with enthusiasm and optimism. Governments and regulators worked towards creating a conducive environment for trading, developing robust regulatory frameworks, and implementing financial reforms. This included measures such as enhancing transparency, improving corporate governance practices, and ensuring investor protection.

While the journey towards developing sustainable stock exchanges was not without its challenges, African nations persevered and made significant strides. Countries such as South Africa, Egypt, Kenya, and Nigeria emerged as leaders in this domain, showcasing remarkable growth and attracting international attention.

African stock exchanges have not only facilitated the listing and trading of local companies but have also opened doors for foreign companies to tap into the continent's vast potential. This has led to increased cross-border investments, technology transfer, and knowledge sharing.

Furthermore, the post-independence development of African stock exchanges has contributed to the overall economic transformation of the continent. It has provided opportunities for wealth creation, job creation, and the development of financial markets and institutions.

As African stock exchanges continue to evolve and adapt to changing global dynamics, they hold tremendous potential for further growth and development. The future of these exchanges lies in their ability to embrace technological advancements, strengthen regulatory frameworks, and foster collaboration among different stakeholders.

In conclusion, the post-independence development of African stock exchanges has been a remarkable journey, characterized by determination, resilience, and a vision for economic progress. These exchanges have played a crucial role in unlocking the potential of the continent and will continue to shape its economic landscape in the years to come.

The oldest African stock exchanges

The oldest African stock exchanges include the Johannesburg Stock Exchange (JSE) in South Africa, established in 1887, and the Egyptian Exchange (EGX) in Cairo, founded in 1903. The JSE holds the title of Africa's largest stock exchange, playing a pivotal role in investment and economic growth. Meanwhile, the EGX is the second largest in Africa and the largest in the Middle East and North Africa (MENA) region.

The Casablanca Stock Exchange (CSE) in Morocco, established in 1929, ranks as the third oldest African stock exchange. Hosting over 200 listed companies, it serves as a significant source of funding for Moroccan businesses.

The Nigerian Stock Exchange (NSE), established in 1960, stands as the fourth oldest African exchange, ranking second in Africa by market capitalization. With over 200 listed companies, the banking sector contributes significantly to the index.

The Botswana Stock Exchange (BSE), founded in 1989, is the fifth oldest African stock exchange. It is the sole exchange in the Southern African region, holding the position of the largest in terms of market capitalization.

Biggest African Stock Exchanges

Among the biggest African stock exchanges are:

1. Johannesburg Stock Exchange (JSE) in South Africa, the largest in Africa with a market capitalization exceeding $1.5 trillion.

2. Egypt Exchange (EGX), the second largest in Africa, located in Cairo with a market capitalization surpassing $300 billion.

3. Nigerian Stock Exchange (NSE), the third largest in Africa, situated in Lagos with a market capitalization exceeding $100 billion.

4. Casablanca Stock Exchange (CSE), the fourth largest in Africa, located in Morocco with a market capitalization over $80 billion.

5. Bourse de Tunis (BVMT), the fifth largest in Africa, situated in Tunisia with a market capitalization exceeding $50 billion.

Challenges faced by African stock exchanges and their resilience

African stock exchanges have a rich and complex history, intertwined with the continent's economic, political, and social development. However, they have not been without their fair share of challenges. From colonial legacies to economic instability, African stock exchanges have faced numerous obstacles throughout their existence. Yet, despite these challenges, they have shown remarkable resilience and adaptability.

One of the significant challenges faced by African stock exchanges is the historical legacy of colonialism. Many stock exchanges in Africa were established during the colonial era, primarily to serve the interests of European powers. This created an imbalance in terms of access to capital and investment opportunities, with African companies often being marginalized. Overcoming this legacy of inequality has been a persistent challenge for African stock exchanges.

Economic instability has also posed challenges for African stock exchanges. Fluctuations in commodity prices, currency devaluations, and political instability have all had an impact on the performance of these exchanges. However, despite these economic challenges, African stock exchanges have displayed resilience by implementing innovative measures to mitigate risks and attract investors. They have embraced technology, improved regulatory frameworks, and fostered collaboration with international partners to strengthen their position in the global financial landscape.

Another challenge faced by African stock exchanges is the lack of liquidity and depth in their markets. Many exchanges struggle with limited trading volumes, which can hinder the attractiveness of their markets to both domestic and international investors. However, efforts are being made to address this issue through initiatives such as market consolidation, improved market infrastructure, and the development of new financial products.

Furthermore, African stock exchanges have also faced the challenge of attracting and retaining quality listings. Many African companies, particularly small and medium-sized enterprises, face difficulties in meeting the stringent listing requirements. This has limited the number of companies listed on African stock exchanges and, in turn, restricted the depth and diversity of their markets. To overcome this challenge, exchanges have been working to simplify listing procedures and provide support and guidance to potential issuers.

Despite these challenges, African stock exchanges have demonstrated resilience and determination. They have played a crucial role in mobilizing capital for businesses, promoting transparency and corporate governance, and fostering economic growth in their respective countries. Their ability to adapt to changing circumstances, embrace innovation, and collaborate with stakeholders has been instrumental in their continued growth and development.

In conclusion, while African stock exchanges have faced significant challenges throughout their history, their resilience and ability to overcome obstacles have been remarkable. By addressing issues such as historical inequalities, economic instability, market liquidity, and listing requirements, these exchanges are unlocking the potential for increased investment and economic development across the continent.

The role of African stock exchanges in economic development and wealth creation

The African continent has a rich and complex history, and one aspect that often goes unnoticed is the role of stock exchanges in shaping economic development and wealth creation. African stock exchanges have played a significant role in driving economic growth, facilitating investment, and fostering entrepreneurship.

These exchanges serve as crucial platforms for businesses to raise capital by issuing stocks and bonds to interested investors. By providing a regulated marketplace for buying and selling securities, African stock exchanges have enabled companies to finance their operations, expand their reach, and fuel innovation. This has been particularly instrumental in supporting the growth of local businesses and promoting entrepreneurship across various sectors.

Moreover, African stock exchanges have been instrumental in attracting both domestic and foreign investment. As these exchanges mature and gain credibility, they instill confidence in investors, which, in turn, fosters economic stability and growth. Additionally, the availability of reliable market data and transparent trading systems encourages increased participation from both institutional and individual investors, further stimulating economic activity.

African stock exchanges also contribute to wealth creation by democratizing access to investment opportunities. Through initial public offerings (IPOs) and secondary market trading, individuals have the chance to invest in promising companies and potentially benefit from their success. This widens the pool of wealth and creates opportunities for individuals to build financial security and prosperity.

Furthermore, African stock exchanges have a profound impact on the overall financial ecosystem of the continent. They encourage the development of ancillary services, such as brokerage firms, investment advisory services, and research institutions, which further enhance market efficiency and sophistication. By providing a platform for price discovery and liquidity, these exchanges enable fair valuation of assets and facilitate efficient capital allocation.

In summary, African stock exchanges have played a vital role in driving economic development and wealth creation across the continent. They have provided avenues for businesses to raise capital, attracted investment, and empowered individuals to participate in the growth of African economies. As these exchanges continue to evolve and expand, they hold the potential to unlock even greater economic opportunities and transform the financial landscape of Africa.

Notable milestones and success stories of African stock exchanges

The history of African stock exchanges is rich with notable milestones and success stories that showcase the resilience and growth of these financial markets. Despite facing numerous challenges, African stock exchanges have emerged as key players in driving economic development and attracting both local and international investors.

One notable milestone is the establishment of the Johannesburg Stock Exchange (JSE) in South Africa, which dates back to 1887. The JSE has grown to become the largest stock exchange in Africa, with a market capitalization that rivals some of the world's leading exchanges. Its success can be attributed to its robust regulatory framework, technological advancements, and diverse range of listed companies.

Another success story is the Nigerian Stock Exchange (NSE), founded in 1960. Over the years, the NSE has experienced significant growth and has become one of the largest exchanges in Africa. It has played a vital role in mobilizing capital for businesses, facilitating privatization efforts, and contributing to the growth of Nigeria's economy.

The Nairobi Securities Exchange (NSE) in Kenya is also worth mentioning. Since its inception in 1954, the NSE has witnessed remarkable transformations. It has adapted to changing market dynamics, embraced technology, and introduced innovative products and services. This has attracted both local and foreign investors, positioning Nairobi as a regional financial hub.

Furthermore, the Casablanca Stock Exchange in Morocco has emerged as a major player in North Africa. With its modern infrastructure, investor-friendly regulations, and a strategic geographic location, the exchange has experienced steady growth. It has successfully attracted domestic and international investors, contributing to the country's economic development.

These success stories highlight the potential and opportunities that African stock exchanges offer. They demonstrate the importance of fostering strong regulatory frameworks, technological advancements, and investor confidence to create thriving financial markets. As African economies continue to grow and diversify, the future of African stock exchanges looks promising, with even more notable milestones waiting to be achieved.

Collaboration and integration among African stock exchanges

Collaboration and integration among African stock exchanges have emerged as crucial factors in unlocking the potential of the continent's financial markets. Historically, African stock exchanges have operated independently, focusing primarily on their respective domestic markets. However, the landscape has been rapidly evolving, with a growing recognition of the benefits that can be achieved through regional cooperation.

One of the key advantages of collaboration and integration is the expansion of investment opportunities for both domestic and international investors. By linking stock exchanges across Africa, investors gain access to a wider range of companies, sectors, and economies. This diversification not only mitigates risk but also boosts investor confidence in the region as a whole.

Furthermore, collaboration allows for the sharing of best practices and knowledge among African stock exchanges. By learning from one another, exchanges can enhance their operational efficiency, regulatory frameworks, and market infrastructure. This leads to increased transparency, improved investor protection, and ultimately, a more attractive investment environment.

Integration also promotes liquidity and depth in the markets. By pooling resources and creating larger markets, African stock exchanges can attract more institutional investors, increase trading volumes, and reduce transaction costs. This, in turn, facilitates the growth of local businesses, spurs economic development, and strengthens the overall financial ecosystem.

The African Union's African Continental Free Trade Area (AfCFTA) agreement further emphasizes the importance of collaboration and integration. With the removal of trade barriers and the establishment of a single market, African stock exchanges have a unique opportunity to align their strategies and create a unified platform for capital flows.

While challenges remain, such as regulatory harmonization and technological infrastructure, the momentum for collaboration and integration among African stock exchanges is undeniable. As these exchanges continue to work together, leveraging their collective strengths and addressing common obstacles, the potential for unlocking the past and shaping the future of Africa's financial markets becomes increasingly promising.

Future prospects and opportunities for African stock exchanges

The African continent holds immense potential for the future of stock exchanges. As economies across Africa continue to grow and develop, so too do the opportunities for investment and the expansion of stock markets.

One of the key factors driving the future prospects of African stock exchanges is the increasing interest from foreign investors. As more global investors recognize the potential for high returns and diversification in African markets, they are showing a greater willingness to invest in African stocks. This influx of foreign investment not only brings capital but also helps to boost liquidity and enhance market transparency.

Furthermore, the emergence of technology and digital platforms has opened up new avenues for African stock exchanges to reach a wider audience. The rise of mobile banking and fintech solutions has made it easier for individuals, particularly those in rural areas, to access and participate in the stock market. This democratization of investment opportunities has the potential to drive further growth in African stock exchanges.

Another significant opportunity lies in the development of regional integration and cooperation among African countries. Initiatives such as the African Continental Free Trade Area (AfCFTA) aim to create a single market for goods and services across the continent. This integration not only facilitates cross-border trade but also creates a larger pool of potential investors and listed companies, thereby stimulating the growth of African stock exchanges.

Additionally, the diversification of listed companies is crucial for the future success of African stock exchanges. While traditionally dominated by sectors such as banking and natural resources, there is a growing emphasis on encouraging companies from other industries to go public.

This diversification will not only attract a broader range of investors but also help to create a more balanced and resilient stock market.

In conclusion, the future prospects for African stock exchanges are promising. With increasing foreign investment, advancements in technology, regional integration, and a focus on diversification, African stock exchanges have the potential to become vibrant and dynamic centers of economic activity. By unlocking the past and embracing the opportunities of the future, African stock exchanges can play a pivotal role in driving economic growth and development across the continent.

Celebrating the rich history and potential of African stock exchanges

In conclusion, the history of African stock exchanges is a testament to the resilience, innovation, and economic potential of the continent. From the early days when these exchanges were established to facilitate trade and investment, to the challenges and triumphs they have faced over the years, African stock exchanges have played a crucial role in shaping the economic landscape of the region.

As we explored the fascinating history of these exchanges, we discovered the pioneers who laid the foundation for the growth and development of African capital markets. We celebrated the achievements of individuals and institutions that have propelled these exchanges forward, defying odds and breaking barriers. From the Johannesburg Stock Exchange, the oldest on the continent, to the vibrant exchanges in Nigeria, Kenya, and Ghana, African stock markets continue to evolve and adapt to the changing global financial landscape.

Beyond their historical significance, African stock exchanges hold immense potential for future growth and prosperity. With a young and dynamic population, abundant natural resources, and a growing middle class, the continent presents unique investment opportunities. As African economies continue to diversify and strengthen, the demand for well-regulated and transparent capital markets will only increase.

It is crucial to recognize and celebrate the rich history and potential of African stock exchanges. By supporting these exchanges, both locally and internationally, we can contribute to the economic growth and development of the continent. Whether you are an investor, entrepreneur, or simply curious about the history of financial markets, delving into the world of African stock exchanges opens up a gateway to exploration, learning, and potentially lucrative opportunities.

So, let us continue to unlock the past, delve into the present, and embrace the future of African stock exchanges. Together, we can build a thriving financial ecosystem that empowers African economies and creates a brighter future for generations to come.

We hope you enjoyed our exploration into the fascinating history of African stock exchanges. From their humble beginnings to the thriving markets we see today, African stock exchanges have played a significant role in the economic development of the continent. By understanding their history, we gain valuable insights into the challenges, triumphs, and potential for future growth. We encourage you to continue learning about the dynamic world of African stock exchanges and the opportunities they present. Together, let's unlock the past to shape a brighter economic future for Africa.